THE RIDDLE OF
REINCARNATION

Walter Martin

VISION HOUSE PUBLISHERS
Santa Ana, California 92705

The Riddle of Reincarnation

CONTENTS

Chapter 1

THE RISING TIDE OF REINCARNATION

Today the writings of various cultic and occultic organizations are proliferating. Edgar Cayce is pushing his "Association of Research and Enlightenment"; Jeanne Dixon has written that we are about to see an explosion of great psychic benefits through the discovery of the secrets of reincarnation; and Jeff Stern has written on the secret psychic lives of Taylor Caldwell.

The influence of Eastern religious sects and movements is also proliferating—Meher Baba, the Self-Realization Fellowship, Scientology, Spiritism, Theosophy, Eken Carr, and Ruth Montgomery's writings. Sensational presentations in national magazines are surrounding us, and polls now indicate that more than 60 percent of the American people believe in the possibility or even the probability of reincarnation.

The Christian church has to take a hard, analytical look at what is called "evidence" for reincarnation, and it must scrutinize the Biblical revelation on this subject. Let's begin by defining the term "reincarnation." *Reincarnation* is not to be confused with *transmigration*. Transmigration is the old Hindu doctrine of cyclic rebirth in various forms: any form of rebirth can occur (including animal form), depending on the activities in a person's past existence. You could end up as a clam or a sea slug, or you could end up in a higher form, such as man! This is all operative through what is known as the "law of karma."

The Western Mind

But *reincarnation* is reembodiment *in another human body*. The Eastern mind will accept transmigration, but the Western mind finds it extremely difficult. So reincarnation as we hear it in the West is actually a redefinition of transmigration. Now we're talking about coming back again through cyclic rebirth, *but only in human form*. The Unity School of Christianity and Theosophy has popularized this teaching, as has Edgar Cayce in his Association for Research and Enlightenment. So the Western mind gets transmigration lightly sprayed with some Eastern concepts and passed off to us as something new. What we're actually facing in reincarnation is an old doctrine shorn of some of the things which would turn us off, and dressed up to look new and attractive. But if we're going to analyze reincarnation, we're going to have to understand that reincarnation and transmigration are essentially the same thing, except in two forms—one for the Eastern mind and one for the Western mind.

Bugs Over Babies

Having traveled extensively in the East, I have come in contact with people who believe in transmigration. I have watched people very carefully lift bugs off themselves and put them down on the pavement, being careful not to destroy the bugs because they want to be sure they are not stepping on great grandmother or great grandfather! I have seen people refuse to eat meat, and instead allow their children to starve, because the cow is sacred, and they might be destroying someone who lived in a previous life and has now reached the stage of a cow. Rats, for example, are permitted to eat up hundreds of tons of food, yet you can't kill a rat because it might be a relative or some other human being. This is reincarnation in the transmigration concept of the East. But when we talk about reincarnation in the West, we think of a person coming back *only in the form of another human being*.

Pagan Beginnings

The very ancient origin of reincarnation is found in the Hindu Vedas and also in most of the ancient pagan religions. The reason people gravitate toward this teaching is because it tends to solve some of the problems they feel they cannot solve in any other way. When we deal with reincarnation, we're dealing with people who are committed to a very ancient attempt to solve some of the problems facing the human race.

When we examine evidences of reincarnation in our day, inevitably the reincarnation is tied up in some form or another with hypnosis. Just recently the newspapers told of a minister's wife who was regressed (that is, went back through her life under hypnosis) until, to the surprise of everybody, she suddenly started to recount her past existence in Germany. She spoke German fluently, which she did not know when she was normally conscious. The newspapers played this up as a contemporary illustration of reincarnation.

Have You Ever Been?

Various pulp magazines, motion pictures, and TV programs (such as "On a Clear Day") have highlighted the modern-day concept of reincarnation. People like the idea that they somehow or other may have lived before. Have you ever been to a place that you *know* you have never visited before, and yet you *feel* absolutely positive you have been there? Have you ever met a person whom you could have sworn you knew before?

No Forgotten Garbage

Now all of these are taken as evidence of a previous life. However, it has been demonstrated by very thorough scientific investigation that the human memory is a very remarkable mechanism, and that the brain's memory banks store everything, including all the excess garbage that we wish we could forget. Nine times out of ten, people who are tested with these kinds of ideas can regress to where the idea originated: a picture they saw or a person who reminded them of something that they had experienced previously, not in a reincarnation but in their life now. This memory has been buried subconsciously, and then later on they meet a person who *looks* like that person, or a piece of territory or landscape that *looks* like that terrain, or a house that *resembles* that house. Our minds are constantly playing tricks on us, reassociating and reorganizing material that's stored in our memory banks. These are solid scientific explanations of how our memory system works.

Parapsychology

But there are some things that cannot be explained away so easily. I don't know whether you're aware of it, but right now scientists are studying parapsychology and all the things connected with reincarnation. In fact, parapsychology has now been accepted by the American Association for the Advancement of Science and is being taught on more than 100 college and university campuses in the United States.

What is parapsychology? Greek *para*—alongside of—and psychology—the study of the mind. Parapsychology is actually a search into the mind or the soul, "going along with it." It's not truly scientific; it's pseudoscientific. But because reincarnation has produced interesting psychic phenomena, the American Association for the Advancement of Science thinks that it is a bona fide field of investigation and inquiry, and this inquiry is going on right now.

9

No Sure Proofs

Some of the things we read about constantly in connection with reincarnation include the cases of children who at a very early age can remember having lived before. When I was preparing this particular lecture, as well as previous research covering a period of years, we stacked up literally hundreds of books and clippings on the subject of reincarnation. As I analyzed our filing cabinets filled with data and reports, I was struck by the fact that certain characteristics were common to all of these things. I was delighted to see that the University of Virginia's Parapsychology Department had been doing exactly the same thing. After examining hundreds of cases of children who had allegedly lived previous lives, Dr. Ivan Stevenson came out with the following statement: "I don't think we have proof of reincarnation—nothing like certainties."

Cosmic Evolution

According to one great believer in reincarnation, Dr. Seminara, "The theory of reincarnation is really the familiar scientific theory of evolution on a psychological and cosmic level." So we are now seeing reincarnation in our own country tarred with the brush of evolution. This, of course, makes scientists very happy, because this view accepts many of the things science has been attempting to foist upon the minds of the unwary. I won't go into a lengthy discussion of the theory of evolution, because that's a totally different subject, but it is significant that the theory of evolution is now being tied to the theory of reincarnation.

Chapter 2

THE PHENOMENA OF REINCARNATION

As the development of the body takes place from simple to more complex forms, so also, say the reincarnationists, the development of the soul from simple to more complex forms takes place through various cycles of reincarnation. Through hypnosis, which is a very ancient yoga practice, people have been regressed so that they are able to talk about their past lives. And some remarkable things have occurred through hypnosis. One of the cases which I spent some time analyzing, and which I think is worthy of analysis, was validated not too long ago in our newspapers and by the Indian Association of Parapsychologists. I checked this and I want to give you the highlights of this case, which apparently defies all scientific explanation.

THE RIDDLE OF REINCARNATION

The Case of Rena Guopta

Over a six-month period Professor Hamendara Nath Benargi investigated the case of Rena Guopta, a young girl who at the age of two began to say, "My husband, he is a very bad man. He killed me. I have a hole in my stomach." The parents of the child were a little disturbed about this, but they thought the child was only fantasizing. But as she began to develop and grow, she described even more startling things.

By the time she was six, Rena knew in detail the events of a previous life. She claimed she had been murdered by her husband in a town far removed from the present location of the child's home. She knew detailed events of the slain woman's domestic life, events that only the dead woman or her closest relatives could have known. Said the investigating professor, "Rarely in the history of reincarnation has there been anything to equal this incredible case."

Reviewing the earlier events, in June of 1961 a woman named Gerdeep Sing, 28 years of age, was fatally stabbed in the stomach by her husband, Suryeet Sing. He was incarcerated in prison for murder for a ten-year period. The first sign that the slain woman had returned to life came seven years later, when the young girl, Rena Guopta, startled her parents with the statement about her husband and her murder. The little girl then pointed to her abdomen and said, "I have a hole, here in my stomach." She insisted she had four children and gave their nicknames. She stated that her husband in her former life had hurt his leg starting a motor scooter. She recalled another occasion when he became enraged because she tried on one of his sweaters.

Total Recall?

On May 27, 1968, most of the murdered woman's family visited the young girl. She was then three years of age. What happened was incredible. When the family entered the room her face lit up immediately, and she recognized everyone. She named the members of the family, and she then traveled to the place of her previous life. There she identified her house, a picture of herself in her previous life, and all the things connected with herself that only that woman and those people could have known. Yet they lived hundreds of miles apart, and the families never knew each other. Two days after this visit, little Rena visited the home of Gerdeep's parents, and there she recognized much of the inside of the house. "That's when I knew for sure that our dead daughter had been reborn in this child's body," said Gerdeep's father, smiling at the recollection.

The Intriguing Postlude

The most astonishing part took place in 1971, ten years after the murder, when the dead woman's husband, Seryeet, was released from prison, where he had been serving time for murder. When he heard about Rena he was overcome by curiosity. He went to her house posing as a business associate of her father, to see if she would recognize him. The child, then six years of age, was terrified when she first glimpsed this man whom she claimed had murdered her in her former life. "He is not who he says he is," shrieked the little girl, clutching at her mother's leg, her eyes wide with fear. "My husband, Seryeet, make him go away, he has come to kill me again." The stunned Seryeet did go away after revealing his true identity and after photographs were taken of the child and of the man who was allegedly her husband in her former life.

Each step of the investigation was validated by the Indian Institute of Parapsychology over a six-month period of intensive investigation of both families, who never knew each other. Professor Benargi concluded, "I am convinced beyond doubt that the girl and members of her family are telling the truth. I interviewed them individually on several occasions. I used complex interrogative techniques. I even tried to trick them. But on every occasion the story remained the same. They were telling the truth."

There are hundreds of other stories, not nearly as well-documented as this, in various newspaper accounts and in the files of psychical societies. What emerges from all this is hard-core evidence that something is going on that convinces some people that they have lived before. I think this evidence would convince a child, her parents, outside investigators, and anybody who pursued the case from a non-Christian perspective that the child had indeed lived before.

The Church's Responsibility

Now what is the Christian church's approach to the problem of reincarnation? Today there are literally hundreds of millions of people who accept this teaching as truth. We see around us cultists and occultists believing this doctrine, and we see continued evidence of great interest in reincarnation as a substitute faith.

Reincarnation came to life in the United States during the revival of spiritism in 1848. It was at this time that a great interest in the spirits was generated through the efforts of Edward Staint, Moses Hull, and the Fox sisters. Spiritism had a great resurgence. Exactly the same thing happened in France and elsewhere in Europe; mediums were popularizing the same ideas about communication with another world. It's important to remember that reincarnation is connected extensively and almost exclusively with the world of the occult. Therefore when people talk about having lived before, we should consider immediately the background, the beliefs, and the motives of the people who are involved in this teaching. I think the Christian church has largely passed up this investigative responsibility, and because of this we have people today being swept into these movements, accepting things they've never seriously analyzed.

Occultic Hypnosis

In Taylor Caldwell's book *Dialogue with the Devil*, and in Jess Stern's book on the subject of her life's search for a soul, there is strong evidence of occultic power and the presence of Satanic influences. Said Mrs. Caldwell, "If I were superstitious, which I am, of course, I would say that two personalities, Satan and the archangel Michael, took over the book in midpassage, but what they are I do not know. Certainly the thoughts in the book are not my thoughts."

Jess Stern, in his book, *Taylor Caldwell's Psychic*

Lives, says that under hypnosis she recalled many past lives, describing them in great detail. We find that under hypnosis people are constantly trying to get information about their past lives.

The Task of the Church

In order to analyze the case of the young girl and in order to analyze reincarnation itself, the Christian has to analyze the subject from Scripture and also from the other available evidence. If we're not willing to look at this subject, if we're not willing to learn about it and speak out on it, then the Christian church will remain silent while the world of the occult continues to grow. Our silence is always construed as weakness on our part. Every time the church doesn't speak, the world of the occult assumes either that we agree or that we don't have any alternative answers. The world of the occult looks down its nose at the Christian church's orthodoxy because they say orthodoxy doesn't answer them.

I maintain that it is the task of the church not only to proclaim Jesus Christ as the Savior of lost men, but also to give to everyone who asks an answer, a reason for the hope that lies within us, with humility and with reverence. If we do this, God is going to bless us. If we retreat from the riddle of reincarnation, if we do not come to grips with it, if we do not answer it, then we will be capitulating in the face of a growing evil and we will be ignoring the questions that people ask. We will also be backing away from the great and true Biblical doctrine of the resurrection, which reincarnation directly challenges.

Why a Foreign Language?

Of all the tens of thousands of people who have been regressed hypnotically into so-called past lives, there are some very basic characteristics which emerge from every single one of these situations. Number one: the regressed subjects speak in a foreign language of which they have no conscious knowledge. *This characteristic is also very common of spiritistic mediums.* Now this is very significant. In the New Testament the gift of tongues is mentioned in 1 Corinthians 12 and 14 as a language given for the praise of God and the edification of the church, as well as a sign to the unbelieving world. But Satan duplicates the divine language with Satanic vocabulary, and he does it through mediums in trances. It is very significant to note that one of the things that frequently happens in regression (when a person goes back into his so-called past life) is that he begins to speak in a language which he does not know consciously.

No Sound Theology

Second, the content of what these people say when they reveal their past lives is very interesting. They refer to God, they refer to Jesus, they refer to heaven, and they refer to spirits, but they *never* come forth with a declaration that Jesus Christ is the Savior. They *never* acknowledge that there is only one true and living God. They *never* talk about the Cross as the remedy for human sin. And they *never* acknowledge the bodily resurrection of Jesus Christ from among the dead!

17

The message that comes from people who are supposedly telling us about their past lives is always the same: it is hostile to the Christian message of the Holy Scriptures. This crucial fact cannot be overlooked in any analysis of reincarnation.

"Did I Say That?"

The individual in regression under hypnosis is usually aware that he is not the person speaking. That is fantastically interesting. The person who is hypnotically regressed to a previous life speaks, yet when he hears the tape afterwards he is aware of the fact that he himself wasn't speaking. Repeatedly the person says, "Did I say that? I never said that." The "I"-ness, the identity of what comes out under the hypnotic regression, is quite revealing. It's missing in terms of the person being able to completely identify with that personality. They always attribute what was said to something else, someone else, some *other* force.

Too Far Back

I find it very interesting that the person is often affected very strongly by the hypnotic experience. Medical hypnotists tell you never to become engaged in hypnosis except in the hands of a trained hypnotherapist or medical hypnotist. Sometimes when a person is regressed far enough back through his memory banks, an inexpert hypnotist may not be able to bring him back to the level at which he started. If you think the concept of going into a coma and lying unconscious in a hospital for a couple of years is frightening, think about being 8 years of age in a 35-year-old body for awhile! This type of thing has actually occurred during hypnotic regression.

Catalog of Heresy

The book *Many Wonderful Things* provides a complete cataloguing of hypnotic regression and attempts to penetrate the ideas of reincarnation, but it also says some interesting things about religion. Let me give you a brief recap of what people who go back into past lives say they believe. There is not just one path to God; you can choose your own. There is no Satan, nor are there demons. There is no hell. There is no personal sin. We are all part of God. We shouldn't get others to believe in God. The Bible is not the infallible Word of God. The unforgivable sin of Matthew 12:31, 32 is indeed forgivable. Astrology is helpful. God makes no requirements of us. Premarital sex is permissible.

All these statements are gleaned from hypnotic regression cases of alleged reincarnation. What you are getting is a theology and philosophy, and this philosophy is distinctly anti-Christian, totally opposed to the revelation of Jesus Christ. This should begin to tell us something.

Intuitive Recall

Reincarnationists like to talk about several different proofs, and I'd like to cite these because they're worth noting. The first is intuitive recall. What does this mean? Vague memories and impressions that you've lived before. We've already discussed this, and it's perfectly explainable on the basis that the human mind plays tricks on itself; we can be deceived by our memory impressions.

Spontaneous Recall

Second, there is spontaneous recall—detailed childhood memories about a prior birth. A person under hypnosis can supposedly recall spontaneously all kinds of things which he would normally never be able to remember. A case like this a few years ago was known as the search for Bridey Murphy. I don't know how many people ever read the book, *The Search for Bridey Murphy*, but it was a real block-busting best-seller. In that book we had the story that proved reincarnation! Reputable psychiatrists and psychologists attested to the truthfulness of the subject.

Under hypnotic regression a lady went back to old Ireland in the seventeenth or eighteenth century. There she spoke Gaelic, she described the coastline where she lived, she discussed many of the customs and clothing, she had a deep Irish accent—in fact, the book was so persuasive that the investigators didn't even wait to finish all the research on her! They simply released the tapes that already existed and based the book on them, and the book stayed on the best-seller list for weeks and weeks.

The Background Check

But finally an especially persistent psychiatrist found Bridey Murphy and began to check on her background. She seemed to be telling the truth under a lie detector, but still he wasn't satisfied. As he reexamined all the evidence, it turned out that Bridey Murphy never existed at all, but was a figment of a child's imagination. This lady had spent some of the early years of her childhood in the presence of her grandmother, who spoke Gaelic and who had history books about old Ireland. The child had spent many hours reading these books, and Granny had taught her Gaelic. She forgot the language and the history books as she grew older, but her memory banks recalled them. Under hypnosis she regressed to four or five years of age and began to spew out in Gaelic everything she knew at that period in her life. Her recall was so convincing that it was taken as absolute proof of reincarnation.

Psychic Recall

And then there is psychic recall—clairvoyantly obtained information. This is what happens when you get information through the psyche, through someone who tells you, "You know, you have lived before." As the person begins to communicate from the spirits what kind of a life you had, where you lived, and what you did, you begin to listen and accept this information.

These are the kinds of evidence the reincarnationists and hypnotists speak about when they discuss the subject of reincarnation.

Chapter 3

THE CRITIQUE OF REINCARNATION

Now let's appraise reincarnation, first from a Biblical perspective and then from a practical, analytical standpoint. As we put these two together I think we can solve the riddle of reincarnation. But in order to do this we have to return to many of the relevant passages of Scripture which quite frequently lie neglected. In our Biblical analysis of reincarnation we should concentrate on three prime areas—the atonement of Jesus Christ, the resurrection of Jesus Christ, and the doctrine of eternal punishment.

The Purging of Sins

The purpose of all reincarnation, we are told, is to purge us of our sins. Why are people born maimed, blind, mentally retarded? Why do people have physical and mental imperfections? Because, says reincarnation, in a previous life you sinned, and now you are paying for those sins. The purpose is to let you suffer now to atone for the past. Cyclic rebirth in the form of reincarnation pays back the sins of the past.

Now Christian theology answers this head-on. We're told in the Word of God that Jesus Christ is the total answer to sin. We're told in Hebrews 1:1-3, "God, who . . . spoke in times past to our fathers through the prophets, has in these last days spoken unto us by His Son, whom He has appointed Heir of all things, through whom also He made the worlds, who, being the brightness of His glory and the image of His Person, and upholding all things by the word of His power, when He had by Himself purged our sins, sat down at the right hand of the Majesty on high." Please notice that phrase in verse 3, "when He had by Himself purged our sins." The word *purged* should be circled in your Bible if you have a King James Bible. The word literally means to cleanse. We get it from an old Greek word, *katharismos*. If you know anything about cathartics, you know that a cathartic is a purgative. Anybody who's ever taken castor oil needs no further description of its purgative capacities! This is the word that we are dealing with here in Hebrews 1:3: Jesus Christ by Himself purged or cleaned out our sins forever.

Jesus Paid It All

It is not necessary for you or for me to pass through cycles of rebirth. The old hymn puts it very eloquently: "Jesus paid it all, all to Him I owe. Sin had left its crimson stain, reincarnation washed it white as snow." That'll never fit there. It can't, because the hymn is telling us that *Christ* is the answer to all sin. *He* washed it white as snow. He did that by the sacrifice of Himself.

The Book of Hebrews is filled with illustrations of how the Lord Jesus Christ has paid the penalty for all sin. I'd like you to look for a minute at Hebrews 9, which speaks of Christ's great sacrifice as the Great High Priest. Hebrews 7:24 tells us that He is the One who possesses an unchangeable priesthood, an inviolate priesthood. Then we read about the high priest of the tabernacle in Hebrews 8. But not till you get to Hebrews 9 do you have the application of what Jesus Christ really did: "But Christ being a high priest of good things to come, by a greater and more perfect tabernacle, not made with hands, that is to say, not of this building, neither by the blood of goats and calves, but by His own blood He entered in once into the holy place, having obtained eternal redemption for us" (vv. 11, 12). What did Jesus do? He entered *once* into the holy place, having obtained eternal redemption.

The Blood of Christ

Verse 14 continues, "How much more shall the blood of Christ, who through the eternal Spirit offered Himself without spot to God, purge your conscience from dead works to serve the living God." The Word of God is telling us in terms which nobody can misunderstand that *Jesus Christ* paid the penalty for all sin. Listen to Hebrews 10:12: "This man, after He had offered one sacrifice for sins forever, sat down at the right hand of God." Verse 14 adds, "For by one offering He has perfected [literally, "completed"] forever those who are sanctified [set apart]."

We know that without the shedding of blood there is no remission, and that Jesus Christ shed His blood, the Just for the unjust, to bring us to God. Isaiah told us that He was wounded for our transgressions and bruised for our iniquities, that the payment for our sins was laid upon Him, and that with His suffering we have been healed. We are identified with Christ through His vicarious sacrifice, His atonement. Reincarnation strikes at the heart of the Christian gospel by denying the atonement of Jesus Christ. If you are born again you do not need any reincarnation or cyclic rebirth. Jesus Christ has offered the one sacrifice for sin forever, and He has eternally completed you and me by His act of sacrifice before the throne of God. This He did, Hebrews 1:3 tells us, by Himself.

Why Suffer in Vain?

You know, it's very interesting that the reincarnationist tells us we go through cyclic rebirth and we suffer in previous lives to atone for our sins. But it's very puzzling that nobody remembers his past life in enough detail to profit from it! So we don't know what we're being punished for. And if we don't know what we're being punished for, we're quite likely to repeat the offense. If reincarnation is really karma, or the law of justice ("as you sow, so shall you reap"), why not protect the person? Why not give him a full vision of what he had been before, with all his flaws, so that the necessary corrections could be made?

I cannot keep repeating the same thing and being punished for the same thing if the karma law is truly perfecting me. Yet this so-called karma law of justice seems to be turning me over forever on some kind of reincarnational cosmic spit, until at length I arrive at the place where I have some kind of absorption into something. This philosophy is classic monism, in which there is only one reality and in which evil is negated. But Scripture tells us that evil is real and is the opposite of the eternal God. Evil exists by His permission, but it is real.

One of the questions the reincarnationists have difficulty answering is, "Why can't I remember my past so that I can profit from it in the present, and won't have to suffer for it in the future?" This very reasonable question never seems to get a satisfactory answer.

The Presence of God

Then of course there are other pertinent verses of Scripture. The Bible tells us that the destiny of the Christian at death is not to be reborn cyclically but to enter immediately into the presence of God. The Apostle Paul, who went into the third heaven (where no reincarnationist has ever been), and who told us what was there, said in Philippians 1:21, 23, 24, "For me to live is Christ and to die is gain [not reincarnation]. . . . I am torn between two things, whether to depart and be with Christ, which is far better, or to stay here, which is more necessary for you." The Christian isn't looking forward to cyclic rebirth. The Christian is looking forward to being absent from the body and at home with the Lord (2 Corinthians 5:8).

The Destiny of Man

It's quite interesting that wise King Solomon described what happens to a man when he dies. (Most people completely forget about Solomon's wisdom at this point!) In Ecclesiastes 3:21 Solomon said, "Who knows about the spirit of man that goes upward and the spirit of the beast that goes downward to the earth?" And just so nobody missed his point, in Ecclesiastes 12:7 Solomon said, "Then shall the body return to the dust from which it came. And the spirit shall go back to God who gave it." The destiny of man, according to Scriptures, is to pass from this life into the presence of God to be judged.

The Hope of the Church

The doctrine of reincarnation attacks the atonement, it attacks the concept of immediacy with the Lord at the death of the body, and it directly contradicts the great and true doctrine of the resurrection of our Savior. Resurrection or reincarnation? Which was the hope of the early church? If you make a survey of the Gospels, and if you study the Book of Acts, which is the early history of the church, you will find that the theme of resurrection emerges consistently. It is the great theme of the Epistles and the constant theme of the early church. In fact the gospel is called by Luke the good news of resurrection. The disciples went out and proclaimed the good news that Jesus Christ came forth from the tomb in His own form and ascended into the presence of the Father. He is our Great High Priest, our Intercessor, our Advocate in the presence of God.

The resurrection of Christ is your guarantee and my guarantee and the guarantee of all mankind that because He lives we will live also. It was not a spirit resurrection; it was a bodily resurrection. It was not reincarnation in another form; it was the identical form. To confirm this, Jesus said to Thomas, "Put your finger into my hand, and put your hand into my side. Do not be without faith. Believe" (John 1:27). To those who thought He was a spirit, Jesus said in Luke 24:39, "Handle me and see. A spirit does not have flesh and bones, as ye see Me have."

The Glory of the Resurrection

There is no reincarnation in New Testament theology. There is no reincarnation in Scripture as a whole. There is only the great doctrine that Christ died for our sins and was gloriously resurrected. Because He has risen, we too shall rise. Christ has abolished death and has brought life and immortality to light through the gospel.

Psalm 78:39 clearly states that we do not return again in this body. David also said, "I shall be satisfied, when I awake, with Thy likeness" (Psalm 17:15). And what a wonderful reflection we find in 1 John 3:2, "It does not yet appear what we shall be, but we know that when He appears we shall be like Him, for we shall see Him as He is." In the resurrection we shall be *like Christ*. The blessed hope of the church is His coming and our union with Him, when corruption puts on incorruption, when mortal becomes immortal.

In Paradise With Christ

There are a great number of passages we could refer to on resurrection, but inevitably we must admit that Jesus Christ died and rose again *in His body* and not in reincarnation. In Acts 7:59 Stephen cried out, "Lord Jesus, receive my spirit." He was not anticipating that as the first martyr of the church he would be reincarnated! He was crying out to Christ, whom he saw standing at the right hand of the Father, "Receive my spirit."

Who can look at the thief on the cross and not hear the words of the Savior, "Verily I say to you, this day you will be with me in paradise" (Luke 23:43)? What a marvelous opportunity to tell this thief that he could atone for all of his sins because on that day he was going to be reincarnated and would have another opportunity! Yet Christ never mentioned that to him, but simply that today he would be *in paradise* with Him.

No Law of Karma

Jesus Christ denied the law of karma and the concept of reincarnation. In John 9:1-3 Christ's disciples asked Him a question. They saw a blind man and said, "Who sinned, this man or his parents, that he was born blind?" Jesus answered, "Neither one." I like that. That is an exclusive negation! "He's blind that the works of God may be seen in him." And with that Christ healed him. And the man testified that Jesus was the Savior. The whole concept of reincarnation is contrary to the Christian gospel and contrary to Jewish teaching. The Bible tells us, "*Now* is the accepted time, *now* is the day of salvation"—not in the future.

When we talk about atonement, reincarnation denies it. When we talk about resurrection, reincarnation denies this too. Yet 1 Corinthians 15:17 says, "If Christ be not risen from the dead your faith is empty. You are still in your sins." Resurrection is our hope. Our hope isn't floating somewhere on a cloud, playing a harp for eternity, as some have caricatured heaven. The hope of the believer is to be *resurrected* in the image of his Savior, to see Him as He is. And reincarnation denies categorically the glory of resurrection.

After This the Judgment

Finally, there is the concept of judgment. The Scripture tells us in Hebrews 9:27, "It is given to all men to die once; after this the judgment." The Biblical teaching is that there is such a thing as judgment, and that this judgment is not tied up with cycles of reincarnation. We are told in 2 Peter 2:9, "The Lord knows how to deliver the godly from temptation, and how to keep the ungodly under punishment until the day of judgment." The ungodly are under punishment until the day of judgment, but the Lord is delivering the godly.

The Bible teaches *judgment on a specific day*, and not a cycle of constant rebirth. We are told in Acts 17:31, "God has appointed a day in which he will judge the world in righteousness by the Man whom He has ordained and has given assurance to all mankind by raising Him from among the dead." God has provided salvation for us, and He has also provided for us the certainty that evil will be dealt with. "To him who overcomes will I grant to sit with me on my throne, even as I also overcame and am set down with my Father in His throne" (Revelation 3:21). Our destiny is to sit with Christ in the glory. And the Scripture says we will judge the angels. Ours is not the destiny of cyclic rebirth. Ours is the destiny to rise immortal in His image, to sit with Him and to be like Him, for we shall see Him as He is.

Chapter 4

THE TRAGEDY OF REINCARNATION

What about the case of the young girl who had all the facts and the information? What about the details in this story? How is it possible for a Christian to answer the claim, "Here is evidence of reincarnation"? I think we have to give a concrete answer, and we can't oversimplify in giving this answer. We need to be as definitive as possible, so that nobody can misunderstand us.

Now you may not agree with me, but you will not misunderstand me. Either the Bible is wrong and reincarnation is true, or the Bible is right and reincarnation is false. It is my conviction, based upon Scripture as well as experience, that God must be taken to be true and every man a liar. If so-called phenomena and data and evidence lead me away from the truth of what God has revealed, I cannot accept that conclusion. Somewhere there must be an explanation, and it is my obligation to look for that explanation, because God's Word tells me that He has always left a witness to Himself. We are to look for this witness.

How About the Girl?

How about the young girl? She was telling the truth. She *did* remember all those things. I believe that every "hard-core" case of reincarnation can be explained as a person telling what he or she believes to be true. After you weed out all the frauds, all the psychological explanations, and all the memory bank tricks, you still have a hard core of "legitimate" reincarnation so far as that person is concerned.

The problem that remains is the *interpretation* of this well-intentioned testimony about a so-called previous life. Where did the person get his information from? The Bible says he didn't get it from God. And the Bible also says he didn't live before, or else the Cross is meaningless. So *somebody else* is communicating information that seems to be reliable. *Somebody else* has lived during those previous times. *Somebody else* has picked out certain case histories. This "somebody else" has been in the business of deceiving the human race for thousands of years, and he is still actively engaged in this business today.

The Ancient Liar

Jesus described this malevolent personage as a liar and a murderer from the beginning, someone who "abode not in the truth." We know that Satan can sometimes reorient our brain circuits, and that he can communicate with us through our spiritual natures and thereby penetrate our minds. How do we know that to be a fact? Very simple. *He does it.* Case in point: Jesus is giving a discourse of what must happen to Him as the Savior, and dear brother Peter pipes up and says, "Oh, no, Lord, be it far from you" (Matthew 16:22). Roughly translated this means, "No way, Lord, don't let that ever happen to You!" But Jesus turns to Peter and says, "Get behind me, Satan . . . for you love not the things of God, but the things of men" (Matthew 16:23). Nobody in his right mind is going to claim that Peter was actually the Devil. But if you examine the passage you will recognize the fact that Satan *used* Peter; he spoke through him and gave him the idea. Because Satan is a spirit, he spoke to Peter's spirit, just as he can sometimes speak to yours and mine. He gets from our spirits into our minds, just the way he got to Peter. And he lies to us in precisely the same way he has for centuries. We are not, as Paul puts it, to be ignorant of his devices.

The Pagan Demons

Think of this for a moment: this young girl, living in a pagan land dominated by religions worshipping the Devil, could have received her information by the forces which govern those religions. The information which she communicated was accurate so far as she was aware, but it was a lie so far as the facts themselves were concerned. She had never lived before, had never been murdered, and had never had four children. *But the information was fed into her mind in such a way that she believed it.* Does this stagger you?

It is possible for children of people who are worshippers of pagan gods to be influenced by the spirits behind those gods. "We know," says Paul, "that an idol is nothing in the world, and that there is no other God but one" (1 Corinthians 8:4). And we are told that the Gentiles *sacrifice to demons*" (1 Corinthians 10:20).

No Other Gods

We are told in Exodus 20:5 that God will visit the iniquities of the fathers upon the children to the third and the fourth generation of those who despise Him. There is no greater insult to God than open idolatry. In fact, the prohibition of idolatry was God's first commandment: "Thou shalt have no other gods before me." In India, where a great many of these cases of "reincarnation" occur, we find exactly this idol-worshipping situation. Here is a child who is born of generations of people who worship gods. Wide open to the influence of those demons, he is influenced sufficiently to communicate information about a "previous life."

Anyone who receives information of this nature is getting it through the world of the occult and by the doctrines of demons. The Christian can be sure that the source of such "information" is Satan, and the result, no matter how feasible and believable, is lethal to the soul. *Satan's presence and power can explain every hard-core case of so-called reincarnation that exists.* How can we as Christians in any way embrace what is so obviously contrary to what God has revealed in His Scriptures?

36

The Final Evidence

Now some people will say, "Well, that's a simple solution to the problem. What evidence do you have to support this solution?" The evidence is that if Jesus Christ's Word can be taken at face value, He is the Savior of the world. And if He is the Savior of the world—and the record indicates that men have experienced this and know it to be true—then there is no need for cyclic rebirth. Christ has atoned for all things. If His Word is to be relied upon, there is such a thing as eternal judgment, and men must face this judgment if they will not turn in repentance toward Christ now. There is such a thing as the resurrection of the just and the unjust, and the Christian proclaims both. His hope is in resurrection from among the corpses, that one day he might stand whole and complete. At Easter time we sing, "Jesus Christ is risen today—Allelujah!" We sing this because Christ is a risen Savior whose gospel message has gone to the ends of the earth. Dead saviors don't send anything anywhere, but our living Savior redeems the souls of men, heals their minds and bodies, and brings life out of darkness!

The False Hope

Reincarnation can properly be called the false gospel of the second chance. It offers people the false hope of eternal life on a cyclic scale, but it never offers them true salvation or true reconciliation to a personal God. Reincarnation has no personal God—only karma, the law of actions and reactions. Reincarnation has no savior; man becomes his own by cyclic rebirth. Reincarnation has no concept of real justice, for there is no judgment day. Reincarnation wants no part of resurrection; it is not necessary, because you are constantly being reborn in different bodies. Reincarnation is opposed to the great and true Biblical doctrine "to be absent from the body is to be at home with the Lord." Reincarnation stands forever opposed to Jesus Christ's authority: "I am the Way, the Truth, and the Life; no one comes to the Father except by Me."

The Agony of Error

Reincarnation cannot answer practical questions. It cannot come to grips with the fact that, while it talks about doing good for mankind, tens of millions of people have starved and suffered and endured horrible persecutions under India's caste system simply because reincarnation held them in a particular caste cycle after cycle, so that it was impossible for them ever to escape. Even today in India and in other lands, people who believe this doctrine allow their children to starve and their nations to plunge into economic chaos. They will permit the rats to live and the children to die. What kind of reflection is this of the God who said, "Permit the little children to come to me; forbid them not, for of such is the kingdom of heaven"?

Reincarnation does away with the dignity of man by reducing him to an impersonal origin. Instead of becoming unique images of God, we become nothing more than constant cycles retreaded from eon to eon, finding neither rest nor peace. For those who are in reincarnation, the gospel of Jesus Christ speaks force-fully and persuasively: "Come unto me, all you who labor and are heavily laden. Take my yoke upon you and learn of me, for I am meek and lowly in heart, and you will find rest unto your souls."

World of the Cults

by Dr. Walter Martin

The Classic on the Cults

A positive study of Biblical doctrine contrasted with the modern heresies of man—vigorous, provocative, and certain to stimulate thinking and group discussion. Now available in two tape cassette albums, the *World of the Cults* gives an exciting and well-grounded view of the major religions of the world.

Tape Titles:

Volume I
Introduction to the Cults · Jesus Christ, Jehovah's Witnesses, and the Holy Trinity · The Maze of Mormonism · Christian Science: Healing, Devilish or Divine? · Spiritism · Herbert Armstrong & The World Church of God
6 Tapes $24.98 6MAR06

Volume II
Bahaism
Black Muslims
Scientology
Unity School of Christianity & Reincarnation
Unitarianism
Zen Buddhism, Hare Krishna & Meher Baba
6 Tapes $24.98 6MAR07

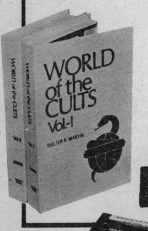

World of the Occult

by Dr. Walter Martin

Are there really churches that worship Satan?
Is your astrological sign a predictor of the future?
Is the Ouija Board a game? Martin covers all the
bases in this intriguing and informative study of
the occultic revolution and its implications for
our time.

Tape Titles:
Volume I
The Occultic Revolution ·
Witchcraft & Satanism · Astrology,
Danger in the Stars · The
Doctrines of Demons · Jean
Dixon, Edgar Cayce: 20th Century
Prophets? · Charisma—Cultic,
Occultic, or Christian?
6 Tapes $24.98
6MAR08 (VOL I)

Volume II
Psychic Phenomena—Biblical &
Contemporary · ESP &
Parapsychology · Hypnotism:
Medical & Occultic · Rosicrucian
Fellowship & Theosophy · Church
of Satan and the Satanic Bible ·
Tools of the Occult: Ouija Boards,
Crystal Balls, Palm Reading, Tarot
Cards & Fortune Telling
6 Tapes $24.98
6MAR09 (VOL II)

The New Cults NEW!

by Dr. Walter Martin

Dr. Martin exposes the spiritually and psychologically dangerous games that modern-day "prophets" are playing with unwary followers.

The Truth about Rev. Sun Myung Moon—A careful examination of the appeal of Sun Myung Moon, contradictions in Unification theology, and Biblical arguments refuting Moon's claims and methods. ■ **Reverend Ike—the Monetary Messiah?**—Reverend Ike maintains that "lack of money is the root of all evil," and he has accumulated quite a following to back him up! Dr. Martin sorts through the persuasive claims of this misleading mind science; one of the most rapidly growing non-Christian cults in America today. ■ **The Way**—This new and burgeoning pseudo-Christian movement is characterized by counterfeit charismatic manifestations, super sales pressure techniques and a questionable scholarship that erodes the basic doctrine of the deity of Christ. Dr. Martin presents a concise and thoroughly doctrinated analysis of The Way Biblical Foundation and its leader, Victor Paul Wierwille. ■ **EST**—The greatest consumer rip-off in years, says Dr. Martin! EST and its prophet, Werner Erhardt, seek to solicit the unwary (for an astronomical fee, of course) in a diabolical system of pseudo-psychological and spiritual exercises designed to "enlighten" the participant.

4 Tapes $19.98 4MAR01

Seven Campus Curses
by Dr. Walter Martin

The seven most common objections to the Christian faith are dealt with, in a hard-hitting, lively discussion on the existence of God, miracles, creation, Biblical inspiration, and other issues crucial to the faith.
Single Cassette $4.98 1MAR371

Do's & Don'ts of Witnessing
by Dr. Walter Martin

A practical, down-to-earth approach for sharing your faith with others. Teaches you how to gain the attention of the cults instead of losing the opportunity to witness.
Single Cassette $4.98 1MAR375

Charisma
by Dr. Walter Martin

The surprising answers from Evangelical Christianity which have been hailed by charismatics and dispensationalists alike as an authoritative discussion on this controversial issue. (From his album *The World of the Occult, Vol. I*).
Single Cassette $4.98 1MAR086

CASSETTE
1MAR086

CASSETTE
1MAR371

CASSETTE
1MAR375